Aunt M and Her Murals

by Linda San Marco
illustrated by Lauren Scheuer

⟨G Harcourt
SCHOOL PUBLISHERS

ISBN 10: 0-15-350681-4
ISBN 13: 978-0-15-350681-9

Ordering Options
ISBN 10: 0-15-350600-8 (Grade 3 On-Level Collection)
ISBN 13: 978-0-15-350600-0 (Grade 3 On-Level Collection)
ISBN 10: 0-15-357902-1 (package of 5)
ISBN 13: 978-0-15-357902-8 (package of 5)

4 5 6 7 8 9 10 0940 12 11 10 09

When Mrs. Kramer found out she had to fly to Los Angeles on a business trip, she had a great idea. "I'd like you to come with me for part of the way," Mrs. Kramer said to her daughter, Courtney. "I'll drop you off in San Diego so you can spend some time with Aunt Morgan. Aunt Morgan would love to get to know you better."

Courtney's aunt was a pediatrician. That is a doctor who takes care of children.

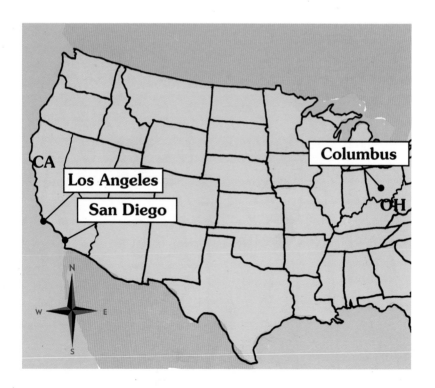

The plans were made, and Courtney and Mrs. Kramer flew together from their home in Columbus, Ohio, to San Diego, California. Aunt Morgan met them at the airport, and she gave Courtney a big hug. Then Courtney's mother caught another flight to Los Angeles.

"I have to get back to the office now, Courtney. This is my lunch hour," Aunt Morgan said as they climbed into her station wagon. "I start seeing patients again very soon. I hope you won't be too bored."

When Courtney arrived at Aunt Morgan's
office, she was amazed at what she saw. It was
like walking into a thick forest. Splashes of
sunlight shone through thick branches. Courtney
reached out and yanked at a branch, but all she
felt was the wall!

Eyes wide, Courtney followed Aunt Morgan as
they entered the waiting room. Now they seemed
to be on the shores of a mountain lake.

"Who did all this?" Courtney asked.

"I did," smiled Aunt Morgan. "Painting is my
way to relax."

Aunt Morgan spoke to Dawn, her nurse. "Did my two o'clock appointment come yet?"

"Yes, Dr. Lerner," replied Dawn. "It's a boy with a sore throat. He and his father are in Room 3."

Aunt Morgan said, "I have to see patients now, Courtney. Please go sit in the waiting room, and I will come and get you as soon as I am done."

Courtney went to the waiting room to read, and Aunt Morgan entered Room 3. The walls displayed a painting of a cute little monkey, offering an orange. The boy and his father were busy studying the painting.

"See this little monkey?" Dr. Lerner asked. "He wants you to eat healthy and delicious snacks." She examined the young patient in her efficient, friendly way. Then she said to the little boy, "Take a sticker on your way out, and feel better soon."

Meanwhile, Courtney had crept into a corner of the waiting room with her book. It had been exciting to travel on a plane with her mother. However, she was not really comfortable around new people.

There were other children and their parents in the waiting room now. Courtney studied them and then burrowed further into her book. She figured she would finish her book, and then she would read the magazines piled on the table before it was time to go home.

After the last patient was treated, Aunt Morgan
and Courtney drove home. Beautiful murals
covered the wall inside Aunt Morgan's house!
Courtney brushed one of the beautiful murals with
her fingers.

Courtney unpacked and got settled. Then she
and Aunt Morgan shared a delicious dinner.

"Tomorrow is my long day, Courtney. You may
not want to come with me," said Aunt Morgan. "I
was thinking that you could spend the day with my
neighbor's daughter, Inez. She is just your age."

Courtney was already a bit homesick and uncomfortable. She said to Aunt Morgan, "I am shy about meeting new people. What if Inez doesn't like me? Her day might be ruined if she has to spend it with me. Please can't I just stay here and read?"

"I have a better idea," Aunt Morgan responded. "Both of you can come with me tomorrow. I have something at the office that I think you will really enjoy."

In the morning, they picked up Inez and drove to the office. When they arrived, Courtney and Inez were surprised when Aunt Morgan handed them each painting overalls.

"My filing room is the last unpainted part of this office. I have already drawn the outlines for a mural. Will you two please paint it for me?" she asked.

Inez and Courtney agreed, and they put on the overalls. They discussed what colors to use. Then Inez and Courtney each painted their first streak on the wall. Both of them enjoyed painting, and they had a wonderful time together.

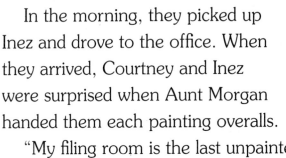

The day passed quickly. Later that afternoon,
Aunt Morgan drove the three of them to the
beach. They spread a blanket and enjoyed a
picnic supper.

"There is a glorious show here every evening,"
Aunt Morgan told Courtney, "and it's free!" The
three artists sat silently and watched as the sky
became fiery orange and then deep purple.

There were many people on the beach now.
They had all come to watch the "show." As the
sun disappeared below the horizon, everyone
clapped and cheered.

"Good night, Inez," smiled Courtney when they dropped her off. "It was really nice getting to know you."

Back in Aunt Morgan's house, Courtney said, "I'd like to stay in touch with Inez after I go back to Ohio."

"I think Inez would like that very much," Aunt Morgan agreed.

The next morning, Aunt Morgan drove Courtney to the airport. Her mother was already waiting for her. "Thank you for a wonderful memory," Courtney told Aunt Morgan, and she gave her a big hug.

A few months later, Courtney mailed
Aunt Morgan a present for her birthday. It was
a picture of a flower, and it went perfectly with
the mural Aunt Morgan had already painted on
her living room wall.

Courtney jotted a note on the card for Aunt
Morgan: "*I hope Inez can come with you when
you come to Columbus for my birthday. I
have been painting a mural in my room. I left
the last corner for us to paint together. Love,
Courtney.*"

Think Critically

1. What is special about Aunt Morgan's office and home?

2. How would you describe Courtney?

3. Why do you think Aunt Morgan asked Courtney and Inez to paint at her office?

4. What is a lesson that this story teaches?

5. What effect do you think Courtney's visit with her Aunt Morgan had on Courtney?

 Art

What Would You Do? Think of an outdoor space that you would like to see changed by art. Design a mural for this space, and then make a sketch of it.

School-Home Connection Take notice of art that is in your neighborhood. It may be a piece of art, such as a sculpture, or it could be a well-planted garden or an advertisement that you think has special color and design. Point out the art to family members.